Contents

Sound and revision

Technique

Songwriter

You probably know all the lyrics of every song in your CD collection (plus some embarrassing ones your mum or dad play). Why not put that amazing memory skill to good use and apply it to revision?

1. Select a tune you know well; it might be something by your favourite artist, a tune from your childhood or a popular seasonal song.

2. Highlight the keywords and information from the topic you want to remember, then list them on a separate piece of paper.

3. Now put together the information so it rhymes and fits with the music. The rhyming words don't need to be the keywords, they can be ideas that link in with what you are studying. For example, if you were trying to rhyme Elizabeth I (the first), it needn't be with aspects of her foreign policy, her religion, her friends or her enemies; it could be with everyday words that you associate with her – worst (at what?), cursed (by whom?).

4. Thinking and playing about with the words in this way will begin the memorization process; singing the song to yourself later on will help the information stick.

Have you been told revision should be done in silence? It's not true for everyone. *Revision* means see again (*re-* once more; *vision* see), but some people prefer to *rehear*. It needn't just be about taping notes though; music can help you relax or remember things.
Here are some ideas for students who find silence distracting.

Application

I began by collecting together some key information from the reign of Elizabeth I, such as:

- 1558 – became Queen of England
- Succeeded her unpopular half-sister, Mary Tudor (staunch defender of Catholicism)
- People loved Elizabeth
- Glorious years followed
- Her reign known for its clever diplomacy, but still had to fight certain enemies
- And so on…

I tried writing a rap at first…
From out of the shadow of the sister who <u>eschewed her</u>,
The Catholic hope called <u>Mary Tudor</u>,
England's days passed to joy from <u>hate</u>
With the ascent of Liz in <u>1558</u>.

I thought friends could join in with the underlined words, but then I tried a more gentle approach using the tune of the nursery rhyme *Baa Baa Black Sheep*. I thought it quite appropriate given that Elizabeth's father (Henry VIII) regarded daughters as 'black sheep' of the family, as he was hoping for a boy to succeed him as king.

A recurring theme throughout her reign
Was balancing power between France and Spain
But in the year of '88
Came Philip's Armada to seal her fate.

What might you put together?

Technique

Rhyme time

Rhyme and rhythm are effective ways of remembering a variety of facts, figures, processes, theories and so on. Just think back to those nursery rhymes from your childhood; you certainly haven't been revising these, but notice how easily they come back.

1. Highlight the keywords and ideas from the information you want to remember, then list them on a separate piece of paper.

2. Now, as in Songwriter (see p2), assemble the words into lines, ensuring the last word in a line rhymes (or close to it) with the last word in the following line or the one after – and remember, these rhyming words don't need to be the keywords (see example opposite).

3. The form you put all this information into is entirely up to you – it's your rhyme. One useful form that most people know (and so is a good place to start) is the limerick.

   There was a young student from school

   Who knew that revision was cool.

   With quality time

   He wrote subjects in rhyme

   And now he's nobody's fool.

4. Remember, the sillier, more unusual or surreal the rhyme, the better.

Application

I like the limerick as an effective reminder of what's been learned in class. Here, I've used it to help remember some of the work of Sir Isaac Newton.

There once was a boffin called Newton

Who had an ingenious notion.

Over an apple he mulled

That gravity pulled

And concocted his three laws of motion.

The First's about continuing on course

Unless moved by an external force:

A body'll keep a straight line

Or, resting, sit there just fine

If a force doesn't mess with its course.

What might you write for the other two laws?

How else could you use this technique for revising?

Technique

Revision playback

The great thing about this technique is that you can have your eyes closed for most of it! All the demanding work is done in the early stages. Then all you have to do is let it sink in.

1. Summarize and organize your notes so they retain the key information while still making sense.

2. Recite your notes into a tape recorder while playing some relaxing instrumental music in the background.

3. Play back your recording, listening carefully to the information. You may choose to make more notes or just concentrate with your eyes closed. Some people find that relaxing music can prepare their brain for learning.

4. Listen to the tape regularly. You may even decide to listen to it as you fall asleep at night, when you wake up in the morning, or simply if your eyes are tired after all the revision you've been focusing on!

Thermocouples are temperature sensors. They are cheap, measure a wide range of temperatures and just about any two metals can be used in them. There are a number of types available for...

Technique

Drama queens (and kings)

If you have an ear for the unusual, or remember snippets of spoken information as if the speaker was saying them in your head, then this technique is for you. Whether it's to memorize a passage from literature or to remember some geological facts, it will bring out your inner thespian!

1. Either select your literary passage to read or prepare a script of information that you wish to remember. You might choose to use a practice essay you have already completed in class.

2. Read the piece aloud in a neutral voice, concentrating on the meaning of what's written.

3. Read it a second time, listening to the sounds and rhythm of the words as you go. Which words would you stress if you were performing the piece to an audience? What tone of voice would you use? Would a particular accent suit it? If it's from a play, what are the characters feeling and how can you show this in your voice?

4. Now, perform in your chosen style!

TIP:
Make a recording and listen to it as a form of review.

Application

Fun with words

Technique

Acronym

This is a popular technique that has been used for decades, where the letters of a word form the initials of other words. At its most basic it helps you to remember rules and lists of items. However, it can be extended through actively thinking about the subject matter to remember a whole host of connected facts that then form a memory chain.

Either:

1. List the information you need to remember.

2. Write down the initials of the keywords.

3. Rearrange to form a new word, ideally related to the ones you are revising.

(See Example 1)

Or:

1. Take a concept that you want to remember.

2. Write it vertically on the page.

3. Find appropriate words that begin with the letters you have written down.

(See Example 2)

Do you enjoy word games, like anagrams, word searches and crosswords? Or perhaps you like jokes that use play on words in the punchline? You will appreciate the fact that the techniques in this book have been developed to re*mind* you – that is, to bring back to your *mind* again – what you learned in class. Who said revision shouldn't be fun?

Application

Example 1

A classic chemistry example for remembering what happens to electrons during oxidation and reduction reactions:

> **O**xidation
> **I**s
> **L**oss
>
> **R**eduction
> **I**s
> **G**ain

Example 2

A more involved example has been developed for a character from Charles Dickens' *Great Expectations*. It requires researching and actively thinking about what is being studied. This is particularly useful when the exam requires evidence to be shown.

Characteristic	Explanation	Evidence from text
Malicious		
Ridiculous airs		
Shrewish		
Jealous		
Overbearing		
Explosive		

Technique

Words apart

A friend of mine recently had a son, but I kept calling the boy by the wrong names: Dylan or Ewan instead of Evan. Having already correctly associated the name with Wales, I needed a way of remembering the boy's name, so I looked for a further association – easy when I engaged with it, as the boy has a (h)Evan(ly) Welsh name. Thinking about how a word is made up will also help make awkward words stick for you, particularly foreign or technical ones.

Either:

1. Notice any everyday words that make up the longer word you're trying to remember.

2. Picture these as objects within the words or make a mental picture of how the objects within the word connect to the word itself.

(See Examples 1 and 2)

Or:

Many technical words are made up from words of Greek or Latin origin. Once you've made the link between these words and how they're used, understanding and spelling them becomes so much easier – but it doesn't mean you have to take up the classics to succeed.

1. Stay alert for similarly spelled or sounding words as you read through your notes. Is there a link between these words? Try to infer the connection, then check the root of the word in a dictionary.

2. Make a word bank using index cards, with the common root and its meaning highlighted at the top of the card and some of the offshoots written below it. Add to the card as you encounter more words from this family.

(See Example 3)

Application

Example 1

This technique can help you remember French vocabulary and pronunciation:

La boulangerie (baker's) – boo-lingerie – scary underwear

La boucherie (butcher's) – boo-cherie – scare a loved one

La gare (train station) – gar – someone with a cold talking about their car

L'hôpital (hospital) – lop-it-all – lop (cut) it all

Example 2

The more visual might remember one of the above like this.

Lop it all, man.

Example 3

Haemo-	relates to blood
Haemoglobin	oxygen-carrying substance in red blood cells of vertebrates
Haemophiliac	person whose blood does not clot naturally
Haemorrhage	bleed
Haemostasis	no blood flow

Technique

Tabloid headlines

Mad, vomiting English men joyously sing under neon planet. See that image in your mind with the headline emblazoned over it and say the sentence again. Why? You've just memorized the solar system's planets in order from our Sun (check the initial letters of each of the words). Silly sentences stick more strongly than sensible sentences. Add the image and you can remember lots of useful information. Remember how you memorized the colours of the rainbow?

1. Either select keywords from a topic you want to remember, or a process that you need to know in order, or the items on a list.

2. Write them down the left-hand side of a sheet of A4 paper.

3. Highlight the initial letters of each word.

4. Write these initials down the right side of the page and construct a silly sentence. Be as descriptive as possible to make it easier to visualize and use a verb in the present tense to give it the feel of a headline.

5. Now picture the scene in your mind with the headline and say the sentence.

6. Repeat until the words and pictures seem stuck together.

Application

You may need to remember the electromagnetic spectrum. Perhaps this headline would be suitable.

What do you see?

Gamma rays	Golden
X-rays	Xylophone
Ultra-violet	Under
Visible	Vegetables
Infra-red	Impersonates
Microwaves	Musical
Radio waves	Radishes

Or you could use this for remembering the six most common German prepositions that take the accusative. Notice this time that, wherever possible, I've used similar looking or sounding headline words to the original ones.

Bis	Big
Durch	Dutchman
Für	Furls
Gegen	German
Ohne	Owner's
Um	Umbrella

Now that you've got the idea, you can come up with better ones.

Technique

Subdivide and minimize

This technique takes association and the use of prompts to their extreme. I found it an incredibly effective way of remembering reams of information for my degree. When I think of it now I imagine it as a word-based Knowledge tree (see p46).

1. Skim quickly through the notes to be revised to prime your brain, reminding it of the work you did in class.

2. Return to the beginning of the notes, this time to read them carefully. As you read, think about how you might divide the information into different sections. This focuses your mind on the material and what it means. On a separate piece of paper, give these sections headings and write brief notes under each.

3. Take a five-minute break.

4. When you return, read through your new notes. Is there anything that is unclear or that you don't understand? If so, check back to your school notes and make your new notes clearer.

5. You've now subdivided the topic into smaller, linked sections and begun to shrink your notes. Will they shrink further? Of course they will! Can you sum up each section with one or two keywords that trigger the full information to come rushing back? Actively working on your notes, as you have been doing, should enable you to do this. If you can't minimize the information for each section into a single keyword, how about inventing an acronym (see p10)?

Application

Shrink your notes down as far as you feel comfortable, checking as you go that your keyword triggers work.

You could go from notes like this...

To this...

To this...

Technique

Story-telling

Some subjects lend themselves well to the art of storytelling. English springs to mind, as do the humanities and foreign languages. But what about science? Could story be used to tell us more about aspects of this and other such subjects? I certainly think so.

1. Highlight the keywords to be revised in your notes and then write them on a separate sheet of paper.

2. Now you may need to think laterally to produce your story. What links can you make to each keyword?

   [e.g. to remember the different parts of the eye: aqueous humour reminds me of water – aqua – while vitreous humour is like glass – vitrify].

   If you're the sort of person who likes to hear words, you will need to think in terms of what the words sound like. This is especially true with jargon or foreign vocabulary.

   [e.g. aqueous humour – the liquid near the outer part of the eye – sounds like an agreeable (acquiesce) sort of joke on the surface; however vitreous humour, which is further back in the eye, sounds a bit like vicious humour which is at the back of, or hidden beneath, the other joke].

3. Decide on one idea per keyword and from there construct a story, either in order (if a process or a specific chain of objects or events) or randomly to hold all the information you need.

4. Watching the story's events unfold in your head may help you to remember it better.

Application

One (strained but effective) story for remembering the different parts of the eye might be:

In the sleepy town of Eye lived a boy whose jokes appeared as if they couldn't get any cornea (cornier). On the surface it seemed there was nothing wrong with his aqueous humour. Not even his muscular girlfriend, Iris Brown, saw through this to the vitreous humour that lay beneath. Iris controlled the light entering his life. That light was focused through a lens in full colour vision for him, but fovea (for fear) of being blinded by her love he used his ciliary (silly) muscles to distort its impact through humour. While his white sclerotic coat protected him against the weather, nothing could protect him from Iris's affections. Ironically, all the nerves that painted the picture of what he saw in her were exactly what produced the blind spot in him.

How might this intriguing tale end?

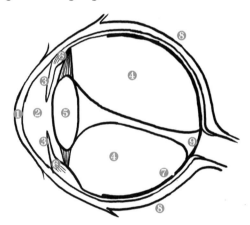

❶ **Cornea:** transparent outer layer that allows light through

❷ **Aqueous humour:** water-like liquid that allows light through

❸ **Iris** coloured muscular ring that controls amount of light entering eye

❹ **Vitreous humour:** jelly-like tissue that allows light through and gives eye its shape

❺ **Lens:** part of eye through which light is focused

❻ **Ciliary muscles:** muscles for focusing the lens

❼ **Fovea:** place of clearest vision

❽ **Sclerotic coat:** white protective layer

❾ **Blind spot:** place where there are no light-sensitive cells, as this is where the optic nerve leaves the eye

Technique

Cause or consequence

Adding detail to your notes can aid recall. This might be exactly the opposite of what you would expect. But is it simply a case of trying to remember every little nugget of information? Well, no, the detail has to be of a particular type and tie in with the idea of making meaning from your revision. And, although the name suggests this might be a science revision technique, it works extremely well with narratives.

1. Skim through your notes on a topic, highlighting any facts that are the cause or the consequence of an action. This action could be relating to a person, a process or an event.

2. Jot down these sentences onto a piece of A4 paper, leaving two lines before and after each statement.

3. Read through the statements and ask yourself: "What was the cause of this?" or "What was the consequence of this?"

4. Add the word because after or before the statement to show that it is either a cause or a consequence. If it is both, add because to its beginning and end to indicate that it is part of a chain of events.

5. Check your notes, textbook, the library or the internet to fill in the blanks.

6. Add the cause and/or the consequence to each statement.

7. Read through your notes again, stopping at each highlighted statement to say aloud the related cause and/or consequence.

> **TIP:**
> Try displaying this information in flowchart form (see Getting in the flow, p48) on your wall where you can refer to it regularly. Test yourself by covering one part of it, saying aloud what's there and then checking.

Application

The example below shows how, instead of remembering a list of facts about a topic (such as the American Revolution), revision can be transformed into more memorable and linked pieces of information that are easier to remember.

Facts:

- America was a British colony.
- Parliament in London governed the affairs of America.
- Colonists paid taxes to the British for troops to be stationed there.
- In 1763 Britain won Canada from the French.
- In 1765 the British imposed a new defence tax.
- Colonists wanted to have a say in their own affairs.
- In 1770 the tax on tea was the only remaining direct tax.
- Britain refused to remove the tax on tea.
- In 1773 colonists overran a British tea ship and threw tea overboard – the Boston Tea Party.
- In 1774 colonists demanded independence.
- In 1775 colonists and Britain went to war.

Repackaged into causes and consequences

- American colonists paid taxes to London because they wanted the British army to protect them.
- Britain was able to rule America because the colonists wanted their protection.
- In 1765 the colonists no longer felt that they needed the British army because Britain had won Canada from the French two years before and now there was no threat.
- Colonists objected to paying any more taxes because they wanted a say in how the money would be spent.

And so on.

Technique

Recipe cards

How precise are you at writing instructions? Would everyone be able to follow them? This is what faces those who like to share their culinary knowledge with the general public when they write recipes. Could you write crisp, clear directions on the main ingredients that caused the First World War or what you would need to re-create another Abigail Williams (not to be trifled with) from The Crucible.

1. Choose a scientific, artistic or technological process, a collection of events that led to an important outcome or a character from literature.

2. Note down the list of keywords connected to this topic.

3. Using the keywords, can you provide step-by-step instructions for someone who has never come across this subject before? Being precise and concise will reveal to you how well you know this particular topic.

4. Write the instructions on an index card, give it an unusual but relevant name and then file it away for future use in your revision.

5. When you read it in the future, does it still make sense? Can you put the detail to the basic instructions when you use Exam conditions testing (see p70)?

> **TIP:**
> You could create a card index in subject order if you find that this particular method suits you well.

Application

In this example you can see how a recipe might be written that demonstrates an understanding of the character of Othello.

Moor de Venice

Preparation

- Take a successful general and soak in a society where some harbour suspicion towards him.
- When saturated, mix with a senator's daughter. This will cause the mixture to elope and return to produce some ill feeling.

Method

- While prepared situation is stewing on the side, mix together the main ingredients for the character of Othello: nobility, honour, loving husband, poetic, a drop of modesty and a spoonful of trust.
- Fold ingredients together and layer with comments from different characters to complete this stage. This should take about two Acts.
- Place on heat and carefully begin to add a few words of the acidic Iago. Leave to stew a little, then add a bit more. Continue until Othello is full of the lies and then bring to the boil slowly.
- Remove from heat and allow to stew in own juices. Taste the mixture while still hot and experience the bitter, jealous flavour that suggests temporary insanity.
- After a few more scenes the mixture should spontaneously combust before settling back into its earlier state, where the taste of the original ingredients will again become apparent with more than a hint of regret.

Chef's hint: check the kitchen cupboards to ensure you know where to find all of the above ingredients (remembering to quote Act and Scene references).

Technique

Formulaic language

If you told my wife about an everyday situation (such as two men digging a hole, with one man having an hour's rest and the other having a rest twenty-three minutes before a third digger came to help them for the remaining four hours) she could tell you a formula to work out each person's work rate – well, pretty much. If you're a maths boffin, why not use your skills to help you remember other areas of the curriculum?

1. Assign codes and symbols to the information you want to remember. Make sure you can easily associate them with the original material.

2. Place these symbols into an equation that explains the plot of a play or novel, a process or a chain of events you need to memorize.

3. Place in a prominent position where you will notice it regularly. Say the equation in its full form as a type of review.

Application

So you need to remember some of the main plot events and themes of *Macbeth*? How about:

$$Am(M + LM) = Pr - KD$$

The result of Macbeth (M) and Lady Macbeth's (LM) ambition (Am) meant that the witches' prophecy (Pr) of King Duncan's death (-KD) came true.

Or how about the causes and effects of acid rain in a more visual formula?

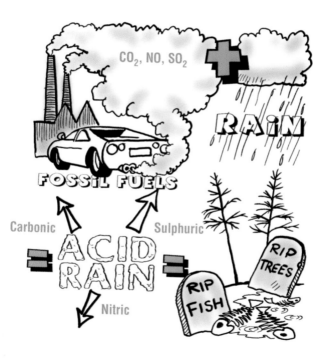

Memory in motion

Technique

Going loci

Loci means position, which is about you linking new information to familiar places. This means that learning can be reviewed even as you go to get yourself another drink or stretch your legs.

1. Write keywords and important (brief) pieces of information on coloured sticky notelets.

2. Stick them on objects around your bedroom or the house (e.g. on pictures, the stereo, TV, ornaments, etc.), making a trail around the room/house.

3. Walk the trail, stopping at each notelet and reading what is written – aloud, if you like. After reading it, look at the object and make a mental picture of the two together.

4. Move on to the next object with a notelet and repeat the above.

For more on the use of position see In your place (p60).

TIP:
Use different coloured notelets for different subjects.

Application

Getting mathematical formulae to stick might be one use for this technique. Each notelet below represents one formula and where it can be used to calculate the variable not given. Where might these reminders be stuck to aid learning? I'd suggest (1) goes on the fridge (cos lettuce association), (2) on a window (tan from the Sun you see out there) and (3) on a poster (a type of sign/sin).

(1) $\cos \theta = b/c$

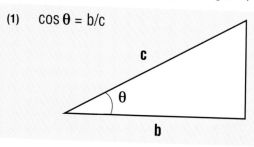

(2) $\tan \theta = a/b$

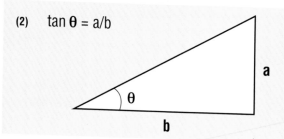

(3) $\sin \theta = a/c$

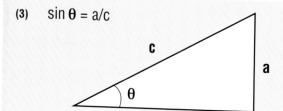

Technique

Walking the line

You may have used timelines before in history to see when events happened and how they related to others. This similar idea lets you feel your way around the revision, connecting time and space by helping you associate events with places in a room.

1. Copy out the key dates for the topic you are revising onto a separate piece of paper and then add, in note form, the important event(s) for each.

2. When you have this information, write just the dates on individual pieces of paper.

3. Arrange these in chronological order on the floor of a room you are familiar with. If possible, put them next to objects or furniture.

4. Step onto the first date on the floor and, using your notes, say out loud what event happened then. As you are speaking, notice what you are standing near.

5. Move onto the next date and repeat step 4.

6. When you have completed this for every date, begin again, this time without referring to your notes unless you become stuck.

7. Repeat again until all the information sticks without referring to your notes. Later, you can rehearse this by imagining yourself in the room and visualizing the dates next to the objects and remembering all the important information.

> **TIP:**
> Draw out as a regular timeline, marking on dates, information and the associated object from that area of the room. Put this on a wall.

Application

As an example I've marked out some key dates in the life of the writer, HG Wells. Running alongside these are important events of the time, which provide a context for his writing. Follow the (literal) steps opposite to get the most from this technique.

1866

1864: Davaine links bacteria to disease

1888: radio waves first detected

1890: gains zoology degree

1891: marries cousin, Isabel

1895: marries Jane Robbins; publishes *The Time Machine*

1896: Henry Ford's first car

1897: publishes *The Invisible Man*

1898: publishes *War of the Worlds*

1903: first powered flight

1909: runs to France with Amber Reeves

1912: meets Rebecca West

1914: First World War begins

1915: Einstein introduces his general theory of relativity

1918: joins British Department of Propaganda

1917: Russian Revolution

1934: interviews Stalin and Roosevelt

1939: Second World War begins

1945: Atomic bombs dropped on Japan

1946

Technique

Movie review

Reinforcing learning through movement isn't everyone's thing. For some people it might seem too close to role play. However, if it feels right to you then it might be worth trying. It isn't about pretending; it's about moving.

You could:

- Talk yourself through an event or a process as you do the actions you've invented for each stage.

(See example)

- Put actions to some of the other revision techniques you've used as you revisit them (e.g. see Story-telling, p18 or Rhyme time, p4).

- Act out a scene in the language you are revising. Don't script it first – improvise. Simply stick some of the important words and phrases on the wall of your bedroom and use them as you enact the scene. Leave them up there afterwards so you get used to seeing and hearing them in your head. If there are two characters in the improvised scene, then play both roles, using different voices.

> **TIP:**
> Use exaggerated gestures while doing any of the above activities. It may feel strange at first, but it should help you build up associations between the words and the actions.

Application

This example, demonstrating the life cycle of a star, can be done using the whole body or just hands and fingers. Add in a commentary as you do the actions – some sound effects too if you feel like it.

Stage	Action
Nebula (cloud of dust)	Move fingers as if tickling something invisible between them
Cloud contracts due to the pull of its own gravity	Clap palms together, still moving fingers
Particles collide and cause thermonuclear reactions, emitting heat and light. A star is formed – our Sun is at this stage	Rub hands together and feel the heat being generated at the same time splaying fingers to imitate the Sun
Hydrogen runs out, causing more nuclear reactions. The star cools and expands into a red giant	Stop rubbing hands together and cup them as if holding a large insect within
The star explodes to form a supernova	Throw hands apart
Original star shrinks to become a dense neutron star	Make one hand into a clenched fist
The star shrinks further to become a black hole, sucking in light and materials around it	Move the fist towards your mouth, which is sucking in air

Technique

Out in the world

Revision doesn't have to be about sitting in a room with books and paper. Escape to visit something/somewhere related to your studies. This will put your learning into context and is particularly useful if you're the type of person who needs to experience things for them to stick more firmly in your mind.

1. Decide where you're going in relation to what you need to revise. You might choose to visit a place from a particular period in history, a building to view the effects of pollution on it and/or the environment, a science museum, or to see for yourself what erosion has done to your surroundings.

2. Before you go, read through the relevant revision. Make notes on what other information you would like and questions to which you would like to find the answer when you get there. Remember to take some spare paper and a pen with you.

3. Once there, observe what's around you or ask any experts (if in a National Park, for example) to answer your questions. Do other questions come to mind that you want answering? Jot these down and find out (you may need to return to your books for some).

4. Handle any relevant objects and take part in any activities if visiting a structured learning event. Notice how you feel as you engage with the material.

Application

With friends

Technique

Teaching to learn

You can't teach or explain something unless you really understand it – ask any teacher! This sociable activity involves you working in pairs or small groups to help each other with your learning.

1. Agree on the topic(s) to be revised and allocate sections to each learner.

2. Everyone now selects a revision strategy of his/her choice to learn their section of the topic (see other examples in this book).

3. When the revision has been completed they must then teach it to the other(s).

4. The 'student(s)' can ask questions throughout and the 'teacher' might check understanding at the end with his/her own verbal quiz.

Many people work better as part of a group. And why not? Despite exams testing individual performance, you are not in competition with your friends. Helping each other to prepare is a good idea if this type of learning suits you. However, insist your group lays down learning rules to ensure peer pressure works in a positive way.

Application

Profit allocation

Ploughed-back profit

Profit

Shareholder dividends

Taxes

Technique

Discussion group

Which did you prefer in class: when the teacher told you something or when you explored ideas through discussion or debate? Revision shouldn't be about learning information in a detached manner – get involved with the issues! Talk helps to clarify and refine our understanding and commit it to memory. An important skill here, though, is keeping the chat focused.

1. Select an area of your studies where there is some controversy, such as an important historical decision, motives of a historical/literary figure, varying sociological approaches to a particular aspect of society, a religious doctrine, etc.

Then, either:

2. Brainstorm naive questions that someone encountering the issue for the first time might raise.

3. Write these on strips of paper and throw them onto the floor.

4. When you have at least a dozen, take turns in picking and answering one. The speaker includes his/her own thoughts and views on the decision, approach, etc.

5. When s/he has finished, anyone can join the discussion, adding views, details, or further questions that occur.

6. The next person then selects a question, and so on.

Or:

2. Agree the different viewpoints for the issue (e.g. the sociological issue may have a Marxist/feminist/ postmodernist perspective).

3. Summarize the viewpoints on different index cards.

4. As if selecting from a pack of playing cards, each group member takes a card from the pile. S/he must represent this view in the debate, whether s/he agrees with it or not.

5. Allow five minutes to prepare arguments.

6. Everyone then sums up their given view in a couple of sentences before the debate is opened up.

Application

Such naive questions as those below on Sikhism can help you check your own understanding of the religion is clear, as well as helping others in the group clarify theirs.

What is the basis of Sikhism?

Where do Sikhs worship?

What's a chauri?

How do Sikhs serve God in everyday life?

What's the name of the Sikhs' holy book and what does it contain?

What dietary restrictions, if any, do Sikhs have and why?

Who are prominent Sikhs in the world today?

What religious festivals do Sikhs celebrate and when?

What do the Sikh religious festivals mean?

How do Sikhs pray?

What is the name of the Sikh headdress and why do they wear it?

Where is the Sikhs' holiest place? Why is it considered holy?

Technique

Describe and draw

Perhaps you've revised labelled diagrams in the past by staring at them and then trying to reproduce them again and again until they were right. Try this more social and unusual technique for two. Again, it's all about active engagement with the revision. The speaker benefits by encoding drawn information into language and rehearsing it; the listener by translating the spoken word into a visual image to be reproduced.

1. Choose who is to speak and who is to listen. The speaker has the diagram and the listener a pencil and paper. The two of you sit back to back.

2. The speaker describes the diagram in enough detail for the listener to reproduce it accurately. The listener cannot look at what the speaker is describing; the speaker cannot look to see how well the listener is doing.

3. When you have finished put the two diagrams next to each other and make any corrections, then swap roles and try a different one.

4. Return at a later date to the first diagram, but with the speaker and listener roles reversed.

Alternatively:
Modify this technique to help practise a foreign language.

1. The speaker has a picture in front of him/her; the listener has a blank piece of paper and a pencil. The two of you sit back to back again.

2. The speaker describes (in the target language) what s/he sees; the listener tries to re-create it without looking. The listener can ask questions – again, in the target language.

> **TIP:**
> Try changing the roles: one asks questions and the other answers – the person with the picture answers the questions of the person who is trying to draw the scene with the questioner leading the revision.

Picture it!

Technique

Concept mapping

Linking ideas, or concepts, has always been important in learning. If you stop to think about it, how would we build up our knowledge without our ability to do this? Here, I recommend a straightforward tool that many teachers have been using for years. You could use it to link the concepts involved in your revision – it should make it much easier than trying to remember isolated bits of information.

1. Using your notes, write down the ideas/concepts that make up that topic (e.g. the collection of circumstances that brought the Nazis to power or the variety of characters that impacted on Pip's life in *Great Expectations*). Write one keyword or phrase per index card.

2. Arrange the cards on a large sheet of paper, turned landscape. Draw connecting lines between the concepts, labelling what the links mean. Remove one card at a time, writing its keyword or phrase on the paper. Repeat this for all the cards until you have a completed concept map.

3. Check back in your notes to make sure you have marked all the links.

4. Test yourself later by writing out some new index cards without looking at your notes or the first concept map.

5. Repeat steps 2 and 3.

> **TIP:**
> Why not stick one of the concept maps on the wall as a reference? You could colour the major links red and the minor links blue to make it a more striking and memorable image.

Are you able to see things clearly in your head? Can you picture your bedroom and where everything is? Would you notice if something was moved? We have an acute visual memory, some people more so than others. This section uses what we understand about this mode of remembering and suggests ways of harnessing it for revision purposes.

Application

A simple concept map links the associations between the characters in Charles Dickens' *Great Expectations*.

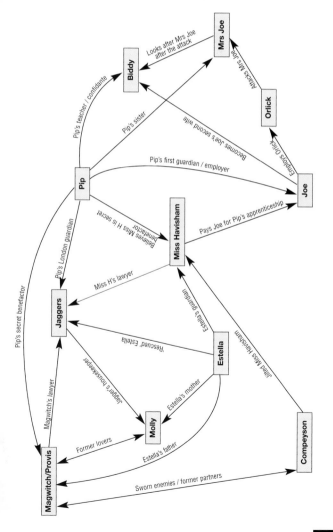

Technique

Labelled!

What sort of images and associations do the keywords and phrases that you've been reading bring to mind? Using the visual techniques below might be for you – either that or they will be a different way of decorating your room!

1. On a large sheet of paper, draw or cut out a diagram that you want to learn, or draw a central image that represents your topic.

2. Then, either:

    Label the diagram with relevant information written on coloured paper arrows. If necessary, write some more detail next to the arrow. For example, a drawing of the digestive system might carry labels for: **epiglottis** – stops food from entering lungs; **stomach** – mixes food with acid and enzymes to break it up; **pyloric sphincter** – ring of muscle that keeps food inside stomach; **liver** – processes digested food; **gall bladder** – stores and passes out bile; **pancreas** – produces enzymes that help break down the food; **hepatic portal vein** – blood tube taking broken down food to liver; **colon** – absorbs water; and **anus** – excretes waste material.

    Or:

    Write keywords and phrases around the image that trigger a chain of information for you (see Story-telling, p19).

    (See Example)

3. Stick the completed sheets around your room or even other parts of the house. Will one fit in the kitchen? How about on the door to the living room?

4. Make a point of stopping to read them whenever you walk past.

5. Revisit them regularly on 'mental walks' around the house.

Application

Remembering lines from Byron's poem, *She Walks in Beauty*, could be assisted by using labels around the woman he's admiring. Use an image next to each line to help remember the quote or any devices used. When looking at the finished picture, the quotes and your response to them should be said aloud.

Head – 'A mind at peace with all below'

Hair – '...the nameless grace / Which waves in every raven tress'

Chest – 'A heart whose love is innocent'

Eyes – 'And all that's best of dark and bright / Meet in her aspect and her eyes'

Lips – 'The smiles that win'

Cheek – 'Or softly lightens o'er her face'

Legs – 'She walks in beauty, like the night / Of cloudless climes and starry skies'

Technique

Pattern scattergram

Linking through categories is an effective way of making sense of information; add in the visual elements of colour and patterns and you have a powerful means of remembering.

1. Cut several index cards into quarters.

2. On each card, write a keyword or phrase from the topic you are studying. Think of as many as possible and then check through your notes to make sure you have all the important ones.

3. When you have finished, group the cards on the floor in categories and give each category a name. As you do this, explain (out loud) to yourself the relevance of each keyword being under that heading. Continue to do this until every card is grouped and visible within a category. Don't worry about making the groupings neat; their shapes should help you remember them.

4. Now put the title of the topic you are studying in the middle of a sheet of paper and copy down each category title with its keywords. Make each grouping a different colour.

5. Look at the sheet, then close your eyes and try to picture the shapes with all the words and colours.

6. Later, take a blank piece of paper and try to draw out the same pattern scattergram, explaining to yourself once again each keyword's relevance and reason for being in that category.

7. You may later be able to subdivide the categories further to extend your revision.

Application

In the example below from organic chemistry, aliphatic hydrocarbons can be divided into these four groups. Any of the groups can then be examined in more detail by placing them at the centre of other pattern scattergrams with their own categories around them.

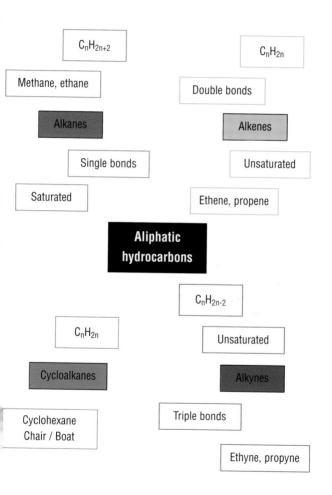

Technique

Knowledge trees

Sometimes known as Mind Maps® (see Buzan, 1993) this technique lends itself well to the tree image, as it consists of a network of branches that allow the learner to order revision in a hierarchical manner. Knowledge trees are the perfect antidote to reams of writing and can be arranged to conform to the 7±2 rule – the chunking of information into memory bits.

1. Take a large piece of paper and turn it landscape.
2. Draw an image in the middle that symbolizes the topic you are about to revise.
3. Skim through your class notes of the topic, dividing them into categories as you read. On your paper, draw a branch from your central image for each of the categories and label them. Keep these to no more than nine branches (7±2 rule).
4. Add detail to each of the category branches by drawing sub-branches off each one with a keyword or phrase that means something to you. Again, keep these to nine or less.
5. Add further related information on the end of each in the form of sub-sub-branches (twigs?). Remember to keep to the number rule again. [At this stage it's possible to have a huge amount of information to be memorized. In this form, though, it's not many separate items to remember; it's up to nine related categories, each with nine offshoots of related detail, of which each has nine more 'chunks'. This is powerful stuff.]
6. Add in pictures or symbols, plenty of colour and then stick it on the wall, where it can be clearly seen and, from time to time, cover a category branch and test yourself. When it's been on the wall for a while, try reproducing it without peeping.

> **TIP:**
> Try looking at the knowledge tree and then closing your eyes and seeing it in your mind. Can you read the detail? If you can't yet, look again at the wall and then give it another go.

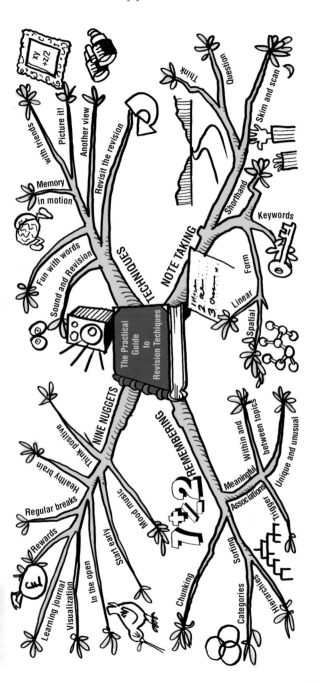

Technique

Getting in the flow

You may have used a flowchart before only in computing or design and technology. However, it can be a useful visual way of re-packaging many other subject areas, in fact anything with a chain of events or that involves a decision-making element.

1. Read through your notes and highlight the process/actions and decisions that led to a particular outcome. Revision possibilities include historical chains of events, scientific processes, plots of novels and so on.

2. Transfer the parts of the process onto index cards.

3. Place the cards in order (including any relevant chains of events that were occurring at the same time, in the case of historical and literary occurrences – remember to draw in the connections between these parallel chains).

4. Copy the flowchart, with connecting lines, onto a sheet of paper.

5. Mix the cards up and try to reassemble the flowchart without looking at your sheet of paper or notes.

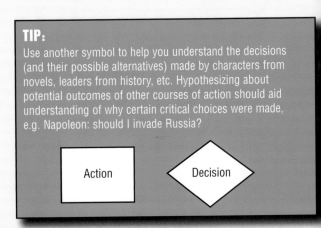

TIP:
Use another symbol to help you understand the decisions (and their possible alternatives) made by characters from novels, leaders from history, etc. Hypothesizing about potential outcomes of other courses of action should aid understanding of why certain critical choices were made, e.g. Napoleon: should I invade Russia?

Action   Decision

Application

A straightforward example of a flowchart can be used to show the stages of Piaget's theory of cognitive development. Other information, such as what characterizes each stage, can be noted on the back of the cards or on separate cards, which then should be matched up as part of the revision process.

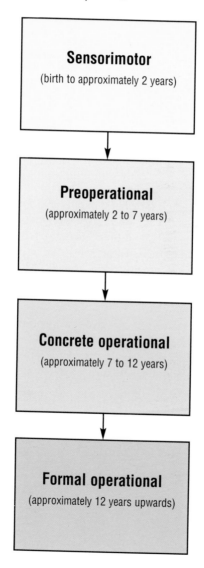

Sensorimotor
(birth to approximately 2 years)

↓

Preoperational
(approximately 2 to 7 years)

↓

Concrete operational
(approximately 7 to 12 years)

↓

Formal operational
(approximately 12 years upwards)

Another view

Technique

Empathic learning

Empathizing with what you want to remember – putting yourself into the revision – can make information stick better in your long-term memory. Adding feeling to learning is a way of putting it into a context.

1. Imagine you are an inventor, a character from a novel, a figure from history or a native of the country you are studying.

2. Look at the events you are revising through their eyes to get a feeling for what it might have been like for them. As you read, ask yourself questions such as: "What do I feel about that?" (a native reacting to changes in his/her environment); "What problem was I trying to overcome with this device?" (an inventor); "What are my options if the enemy decides to attack here?" (a historical figure).

3. The next stage is to check your learning by closing your books and writing a diary entry or a speech about those events as if you are that character. Use as many keywords and draw on as much information as you can.

It never hurts to see things from a different perspective. Viewing well-known materials from a different standpoint can give you a whole new take on them. And that 'new take' involves not just other standpoints, but other sprawled-out and sitting points as well. You'll see.

Application

This example imagines the diary of Fritz Haber, the inventor of the Haber Process for ammonia production.

Before

I was amazed to hear recently that we rely on Chilean bird droppings as the source of the world's ammonia! What did they say, that this sludge is over 200 miles long and five feet deep? Here's an intriguing problem to be solved, the solution for which would have so many benefits, not least freeing us all from this ever-shrinking toilet. Where to start, though? Perhaps with the two constituents: hydrogen and nitrogen – it's good that there's a plentiful supply of both and that they're relatively inexpensive. In theory, the decomposition of ammonia into its elements is reversible. But how might I bring them together in the first place? What temperature would be needed? Would I need a catalyst?

During

The experiments are showing some very strange results. Normally the high temperature gives good yield (I'm currently trying 450°C), but here it is giving low yield. What's going on? Should I repeat the experiment? Surely not; everything is correct, so why these results? Perhaps I should look at the pressure.

After

I've done it! I used a pressure of 200 atm with the 450°C, as well as iron as a catalyst, and, yes, the process is reversible: $N_2 + 3H_2 = 2NH_3$. Any more pressure and it will cost too much to build a plant – that's as far as I'll get involved in the practical side; I'll let the industrialists take over from here. What I do know, though, is that it will satisfy an important economic need and make us less dependent on others. I wonder what the Kaiser will say…

Technique

Order in the ranks

Engage with the information by organizing it.

1. Using your notes, write key pieces of information to remember on separate index cards.

2. Spread the cards out and ask yourself: "Which is the most important point to remember?" Place this card to one side.

3. Continue as in step 2 with the next most essential point, working your way down the order of importance until all the cards have been put in rank order. Should you be undecided between two or three cards, put them next to each other. Your order may look something like this:

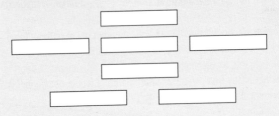

4. For each placing, ask yourself: "Why is this information more/less important than the one above/below?" This will engage your brain more deeply with what's in front of you.

5. Rearrange any of the ranking as necessary.

6. Write down your final rank order with the explanation for each placing. All this engagement – weighing up, deciding and checking – should help the topic stick.

7. Extend your thinking further by imagining how another person might see it differently.

TIP:
Use ordering to weigh up arguments about issues you've studied.

Application

What are the main advantages of using ICT, such as computer-aided design (CAD) and computer-aided manufacture (CAM), in manufacturing? A student might arrive at the order below but can s/he support this ranking?

Flexible to demands

Reduces time spent on design and manufacture

Controls machinery

Supervises production processes constantly

Consistent quality for consumer

Makes costing a product more accurate

Communicates manufacturing information worldwide

Shares up-to-date information with other departments

Monitors work environment

Technique

Venn to explore

You may have encountered Venn diagrams in maths, but they can be used in any subject to show relationships between people, places, objects, processes, words, theories – the list goes on and on. If organization and associations are important parts of your revision, then knowing how to use a Venn diagram is worthwhile.

1. Take the information you want to revise, write it on index cards and divide it into categories using any one criteria.

2. Ask yourself: "What other aspects do any of these pieces of information have in common?" Move the cards within their categories so those of other categories that share a different criterion are near each other.

3. Draw several interlocking circles on a large sheet of paper and label each one. Arrange each card either entirely within one category (if it doesn't share any features with another category), or place it within an overlap between two (or three, etc.) categories. The diagram below shows how information might be arranged within three circles.

4. When you are happy with your categories, copy the information into your drawing of the circles.

5. Explain to someone (or aloud to yourself) why you have divided the information like that and what it means. What else can you tell your listener about the items in the circles?

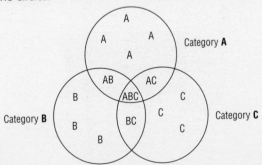

Application

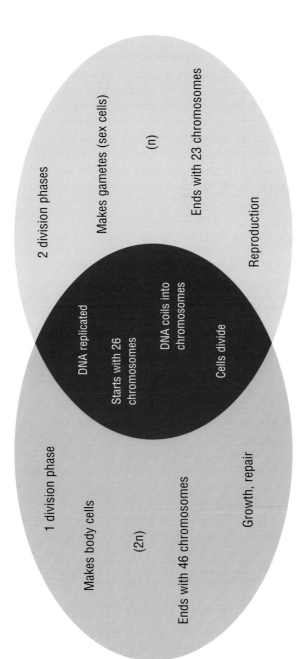

Mitosis

Meiosis

- 1 division phase
- 2 division phases
- Makes body cells
- Makes gametes (sex cells)
- (2n)
- (n)
- Ends with 46 chromosomes
- Ends with 23 chromosomes
- Growth, repair
- Reproduction

Shared (overlap):
- DNA replicated
- Starts with 26 chromosomes
- DNA coils into chromosomes
- Cells divide

Technique

PASS master

For those of you who prefer a more traditional approach, this is a way of directing your reading while paying attention to effective ways of encoding information for memory. Based on the well-known PQRST (Preview, Question, Read, Self-recitation, Test) method (Thomas and Robinson, 1982), it encourages you to remember through organizing the material and by making good use of the auditory route to memory. Keeping with the ethos of memory tips, I've used an appropriate acronym to help you remember the steps to success.

1. **P**repare your notes for revision by dividing them into different sections and assigning these headings. Write each heading on a blank side of paper.

2. **A**sk yourself questions that you think each section of your notes should answer. These should be quality questions, that is, who, what, where, when, why and how, as they open up your thinking. Jot these down under each of your headings.

3. **S**can your notes for the answers.

4. **S**ay and note the answers as you encounter them. Ask yourself: "How does this link to what has gone before and to what I already know?" Note down this response too.

5. When you have finished answering all the questions, read through them once more, saying and rephrasing what you have discovered, while paying attention to the headings the answers are under.

6. Check how much you've remembered by using one of the other techniques in this book.

Application

Here's how it might work when revising the book *Of Mice and Men*:

Prepare

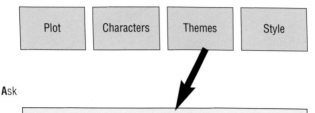

Plot	Characters	Themes	Style

Ask

Themes

1. What are the main themes?

2. How are these themes revealed?

3. Which characters relate to each and how?

Scan

Say

> *Key theme: dreams... particularly recurring 'American Dream' of George and Lennie – want to better themselves and own land...*

Technique

In context

This technique refers to the context of the events you're revising. You'll get a more interesting and full perspective on the material when all the factual pieces are put together.

1. Read around the background of your topic.

2. Ask yourself:

   ■ how what you are studying was affected by the context in which it took place (e.g. the period a writer was living in may affect his/her writing and the attitudes reflected in it; a historical figure may be swayed by what s/he sees around her/him; or the development of a country may have been influenced by its natural resources).

   ■ how it affected the context (e.g. what was the writer's effect on his/her world – did the social morals of the writing make a difference to society? How did a historical figure's conquest affect the country in years to come? Or how did a country's use of its natural resources impact on its environment?)

3. Use one of the other techniques in the book to rehearse this information (see Getting in the flow, p48).

Application

The Second World War was a horrific and devastating war in all kinds of ways. Yet today we use, or even depend on, the updated versions of some of those discoveries and inventions. The need to triumph over the enemy speeded up advancement as it had done in previous wars. Below is an example from the Second World War of how the paths of history and science cross.

Discovery / invention	In war	In peace
Radar	Used to detect enemy planes. Proved crucial in the UK's triumph over Germany in the Battle of Britain	1. Still used in and with aircraft – military and commercial 2. Weather forecasting 3. Police speed checks
Jet engine	Discovered in UK and Germany at about same time. In use by end of war	Now used on commercial and military planes
Long-range rockets	German invention, used to power the devastating V2s	Technology used in American and Russian space programmes
Splitting the uranium atom	First achieved by Germans, but developed by US Manhattan Project. First successful explosion of atomic bomb in July 1945. Within a month it had been used on two Japanese cities	Before the end of the following decade both the US and UK were using electricity supplied by a nuclear reactor

Technique

In your place

There's something about where we learn information. We appear to make associations between our environment and the material. Even now, so many years after first hearing of (what was then) the Common Market (now the European Union), I can still remember the classroom, its displays and the teacher moving around the groups as we worked on our particular country.

1. Select different places in your house to revise different subjects. You can use the same room more than once for different subjects

   Areas of the house:

   e.g.   Sociology   sofa in living room

          English   kitchen table

          RE   beanbag in bedroom.

2. Before you begin each study session, take a look around you and notice the details of your surroundings from that perspective. Close your eyes and re-create the scene.

3. Open your eyes and begin revising using one of the other techniques in this book.

If you stick to these areas, then when you're in the exam you can mentally revisit your chosen revision places and, with strong enough associations, experience again your revision practice and feelings for that subject.

> **TIP:**
> If you like, and are used to, essential oils then use one for each revision area. In the exam, aid recall with the smell of the oil on a handkerchief. Smell is one of the most powerful triggers of memory (Carter, 2000).

Application

RE – beanbag in bedroom

Sociology – sofa in living room

English – kitchen table

Revisit the revision

Technique

Self-challenge

This straightforward review can be prepared while you're revising a piece of work for the first time. Once it's ready you can dip into it anytime and anywhere.

1. You've just used one of the other revision techniques in this book to revise a topic. While your brain is still switched on to this particular subject, jot down a few questions that your notes answered (e.g. what is Newton's First Law?).

2. Write down the answers to these questions.

3. Scan back over your notes. Check the answers to your questions and write out any questions and answers you might have missed. So far, you have completed one form of review.

4. The next stage is to take a set of index cards and copy one of the questions onto the front of each and put its answer on the back.

5. Shuffle the pile, put an elastic band around them and set them aside.

6. Whenever you need to test yourself, simply select a card at random and answer the question (either by saying it aloud or by writing it down). You could do this on your own or ask others to test you.

7. Note where any gaps in your knowledge are revealed and go back and revise this area again.

8. With the answers you do get right, can you link them together into a meaningful whole, as you would need to in an essay on the subject? You don't need to write the essay now, but might choose another technique to plan it (see Knowledge trees, p46 or Getting in the flow, p48).

Revision wouldn't stick for long without rehearsal, so come back to it time and time again. If you revisit it using different approaches and can still recall the information, chances are that you're ready. All the techniques in this book can be used or adapted to rehearse your revision; this section adds to that repertoire.

Application

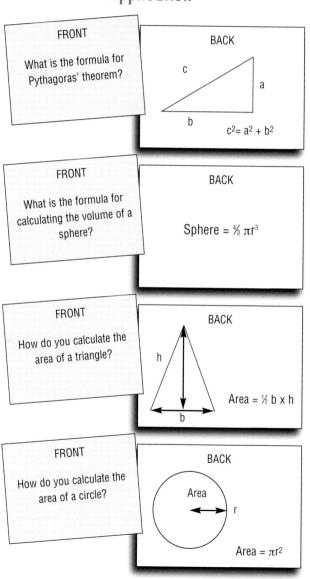

FRONT

What is the formula for Pythagoras' theorem?

BACK

$c^2 = a^2 + b^2$

FRONT

What is the formula for calculating the volume of a sphere?

BACK

Sphere = $\frac{4}{3}\pi r^3$

FRONT

How do you calculate the area of a triangle?

BACK

Area = $\frac{1}{2}$ b x h

FRONT

How do you calculate the area of a circle?

BACK

Area = πr^2

Technique

Pro and con cards

This technique involves using index cards to test yourself on the pros and cons of the topic you've revised. If you know the arguments for and against something, then you'll probably know a lot more about that area.

1. Read through your notes, highlighting/thinking about the pros and cons of a particular process, theory, application or decision (e.g. hydro-electric power or the 1944 Education Act).

2. Note each one on an index card, colouring the corner either green or red, depending upon whether it is a pro or a con (see example).

3. Either:

   a. Test yourself and then check your answers using the cards;

   Or:

   b. Select two or three cards at random, lay them out according to whether they are pros or cons and then recite which are missing within each category;

   Or:

   c. Take one card at a time, place it in front of you according to whether it is a pro or a con and then say aloud why it is a positive or negative point;

   Or:

   d. Mix together the pros and cons for all the related theories, methods or whatever you're recalling. So, for example, you might shuffle together all the cards containing positives and negatives for every Education Act you're testing yourself on. Next, take the top card, place it under a heading for the relevant Act and explain its significance.

4. Whichever method you use, ensure that you look at the cards laid out when you have finished and then close your eyes, holding that image in your mind.

Application

What colour do you think the corners of these cards on some of the main points of the 1944 Education Act should be? Why? Would any fall into both categories?

Three stage education: primary, secondary and FE

Raised the school leaving age to 15

Minister of Education appointed

RE compulsory for all pupils

Technique

Key point cards

Similar to Pro and con cards (see p64), this technique also makes use of index cards and is a great way of revisiting the main points of your studies. The actual making of the resource is part of the process of revising and it can be used again and again in a variety of ways.

1. Read through your notes, highlighting the key points to remember about a historical figure or event, themes of a literary text, a particular process, theory, application or decision.

2. Write the title on one side of an index card (e.g. themes in *Othello*) and, on the back, write down the key points to remember.

3. Shuffle the cards and test yourself by taking a card and saying out loud what is on the back. Check your answers.

4. Then,

   Either: stick the cards (either way facing out) onto your wall where they can be seen easily. Test yourself from time to time by saying what's on the back of the card.

   Or: arrange the cards in a filing system. Ensure the system has a logical order so you can go straight to the one(s) you want to test yourself on.

5. At a later date, you might choose to write one key point per card, to which extra information can then be added (e.g. quotes from *Othello* that support the theme of appearance and reality). Again, these could be stored in a filing system or stuck to the walls of your room.

> **TIP:**
> Arrange the single key point cards into knowledge trees or concept maps to show their connection with each other. Copy out the visuals when you have finished and then try to picture them in your head.

Application

This example concentrates on classical conditioning, first studied by the Russian physiologist, Ivan Pavlov.

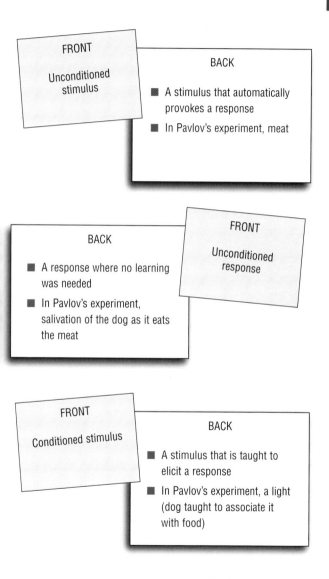

FRONT

Unconditioned stimulus

BACK

■ A stimulus that automatically provokes a response

■ In Pavlov's experiment, meat

BACK

■ A response where no learning was needed

■ In Pavlov's experiment, salivation of the dog as it eats the meat

FRONT

Unconditioned response

FRONT

Conditioned stimulus

BACK

■ A stimulus that is taught to elicit a response

■ In Pavlov's experiment, a light (dog taught to associate it with food)

And so on.

Technique

Opinion dominion

Revision shouldn't necessarily be an emotional vacuum. We all have opinions about a range of issues and certain subjects cry out for some sort of emotional engagement. You need to understand the facts and be able to support your feelings with reference to the material. Be careful, though – only give your personal responses and supported opinions if the examiner asks for them.

1. Write out three types of question cards (as below or similar). Make more than one of each.

2. Shuffle them and scatter them face down in front of you.

3. Review your notes, visual aids or recordings for a particular topic. As you do, note down on separate viewpoint cards areas of controversy or aspects that could have an alternative view (e.g. religion provides a moral code). Shuffle these and place in a pile next to you.

4. Select a question card and a viewpoint card from the pile next to you.

5. Consider and then say your response, taking the view that's been selected. Is there any support for this view that you can refer to without further reading?

6. Repeat steps 4 and 5 for the next card.

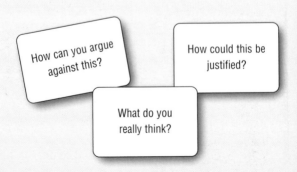

How can you argue against this?

How could this be justified?

What do you really think?

Application

Here, in-depth knowledge of a text from literature is thoroughly tested using the Opinion dominion technique. The viewpoint cards could read as follows for the play *An Inspector Calls*:

Mrs Birling is most to blame for the death of Eva

It's unlikely anyone would have changed if the suicide had proved to be a hoax

The playwright leaves little for the actors to develop in their characters

The younger characters show hope for the future

Mr Birling did feel some regret

Inspector Goole led each of the characters into a trap

The play is about class war

The playwright is lecturing the audience on how they should behave

Eva really brought the bad luck upon herself

Technique

Exam conditions testing

This is one that you may have already done in class, but is an excellent test of recall for yourself nearer the exams. It is best to let everyone in the house know that you don't want to be disturbed for the next hour. Unplug any nearby phones and switch off your mobile as well.

1. Ask your teacher to set an exam question for you, or use one from a previous year's exam paper.
2. Write the question at the top of a sheet of paper, set an alarm clock for the time you will have for such a question in the exam and then begin.
3. When the time starts, only then can you begin to plan and answer your question.

Planning

■ Planning your answer is important when writing an essay, as it enables you to demonstrate all your relevant knowledge in a good order. You may also find that it helps you to recall what you've revised. You could plan using a knowledge tree (see p46) or perhaps reverse the subdivide and minimize technique (see p16). Give some thought beforehand to whatever you think will work best for you and then practise that technique.

Timing

■ It is important that you don't overrun, nor finish so early that you haven't had time to answer the question fully. Keep an eye on the clock.

Feedback

■ Ask your teacher to give you an idea of how you have done. If that's not possible, then check what you have written against your notes, making sure that the content is accurate and relevant to the question.

> **TIP:**
> Make sure you know the exam rubric – its layout, timings and spread of marks – before you begin revising. It will help guide your study and be especially useful when practising parts of the exam, as in this technique.

Application

Feedback

Planning

The Practical Guide to Revision Techniques

TECHNIQUES

NOTE TAKING

- Think
- Question
- Skim and scan
- Shorthand
- Keywords
- Form
  - Linear
  - Spatial

NINE NUGGETS

- Revisit the revision
- Another view
- Picture it!
- with friends
- Memory in motion
- Fun with words
- Sound and Revision
- Think positive
- Healthy brain
- Regular breaks
- Rewards
- Learning Journal
- Visualization
- In the open
- Start early
- Mood music

REMEMBERING

- Meaningful
  - Within and between topics
- Associations
  - Unique and unusual
- Sorting
  - Categories
  - Chunking
  - Hierarchies

$\frac{1+2}{2}$

$\frac{xy}{+2/2}$

Timing

Nine nuggets

Start early

Like many students I began my revision two/three months before my first exam – it leaves a lot to do! It's not the end of the world if you've let it get that late, but it's time to get moving. At university – when I'd got revision sorted – I eased the learning burden by spending an hour most evenings going over my notes from the day. I'd repackage them in some way and revisit them in the following weeks, drawing any links to content I'd learned since. When I came to revise, everything was easier and less pressured. I got a first class degree (and with no impact on my social life!). Compare that to my O levels, where I scraped five passes. What a difference a few years and a little understanding about effective learning make! Do yourself a favour and start early.

Mood music

Will a rock anthem lift you, rap chill you out or soul have you reaching for the tissues? You're probably aware of the effect music can have on your mood, so why not use this? In your breaks play your favourite appropriate music to get in the mood for revision. You might prefer to listen to music as you work, rather than studying in silence. You will find the music that suits you best, although you may find that music that corresponds to the resting heart rate (about 60-70 beats per minute) eases you into the most receptive state for revision. It can also help you relax before an exam.

In the open

The sounds of nature help some people relax into their studies. Perhaps you have a CD of natural sounds (e.g. the sea, birds) that you can play as you revise. Or, weather permitting, you could try revising out in the open. In the exam room, if you start to feel tense, think back to the bright afternoons you spent revising in the open air and remember how you felt. This brief visualization may make you feel calmer and trigger memories of what you were studying at the time.